SECRETS OF THE HUMAN BODY

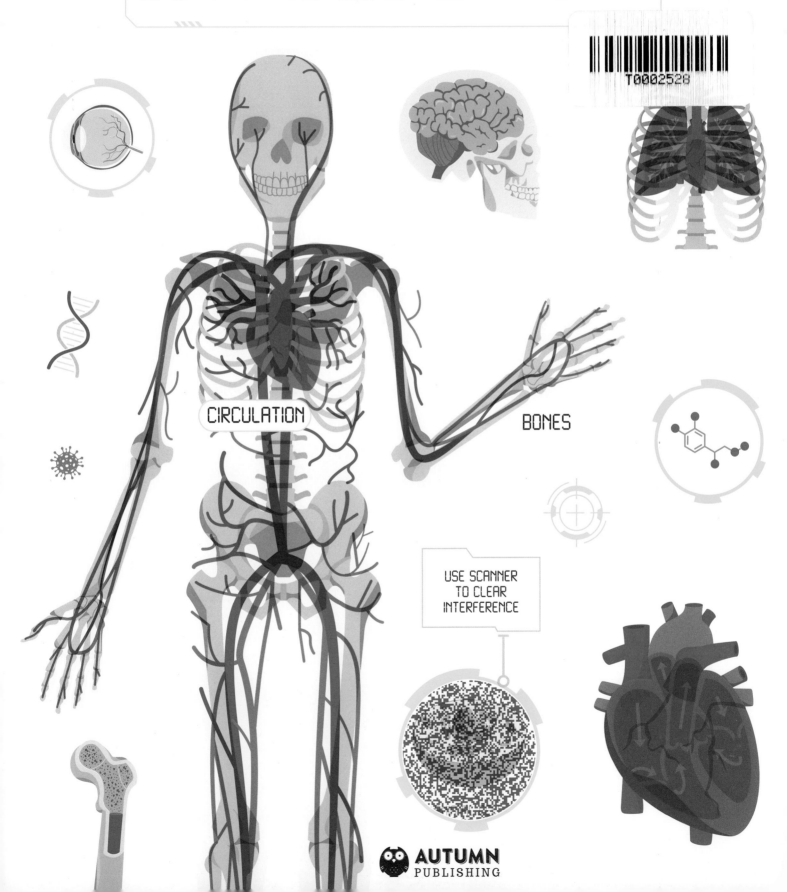

CIRCULATION

BONES

USE SCANNER
TO CLEAR
INTERFERENCE

T0002528

AUTUMN
PUBLISHING

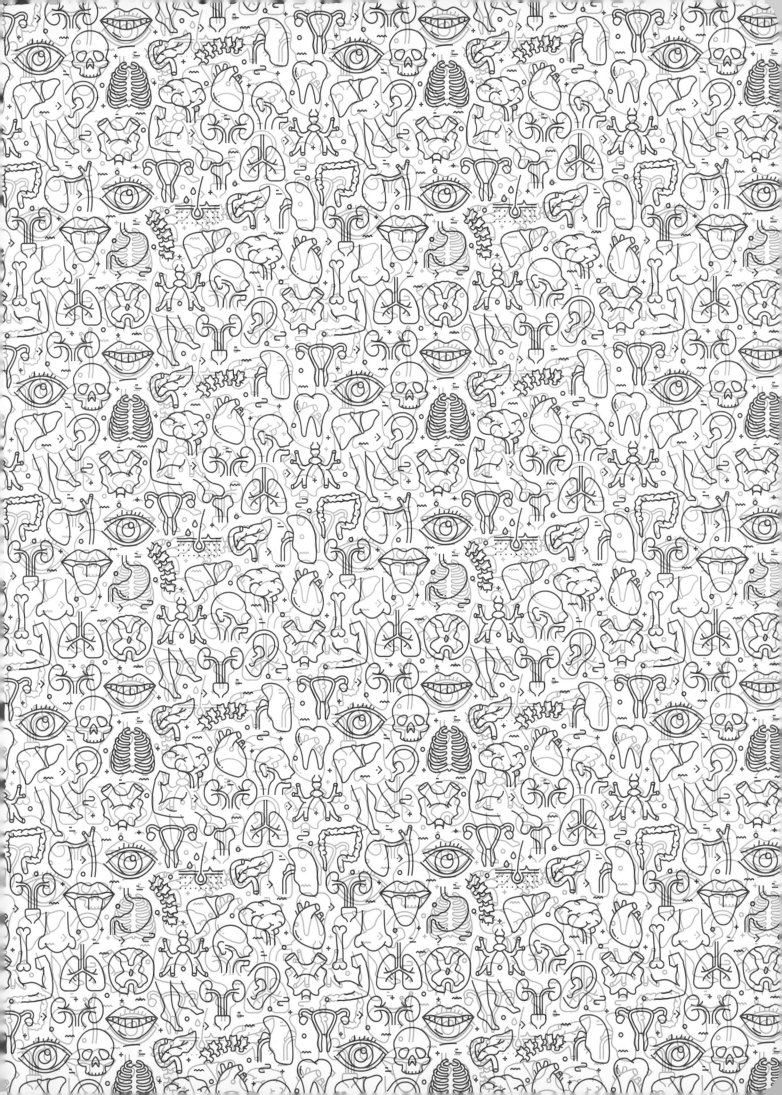

AUTUMN
PUBLISHING

Illustrated by Chelsey Farris and Jake Hill
Written by Rose Harkness

Designed by Richard Sykes and Jamie Abraham
Edited by Katie Taylor

Copyright © 2023 Igloo Books Ltd

Published in 2023
First published in the UK by Autumn Publishing
An imprint of Igloo Books Ltd
Cottage Farm, NN6 0BJ, UK
Owned by Bonnier Books
Sveavägen 56, Stockholm, Sweden

Manufactured in China. 0723 001
10 9 8 7 6 5 4 3 2 1

Library of Congress Cataloging-in-Publication
Data is available upon request.

ISBN 978-1-83771-666-1
autumnpublishing.co.uk
bonnierbooks.co.uk

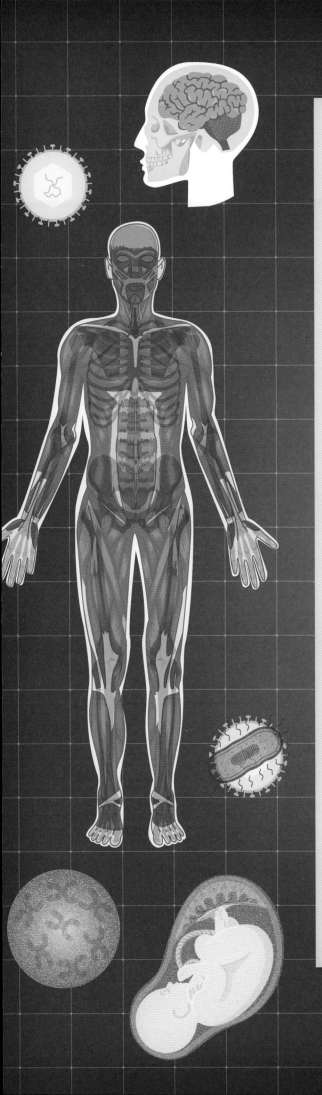

CONTENTS

INTRODUCTION

The human body is like a powerful machine, strong enough to last you your whole life. It has multiple systems to keep it running well, from your skeleton to your nerves to the muscles that keep you up and moving. They're all essential to human life.

BRAIN
Your brain is like a computer for your body. It works 24/7 to control what you do.

HEART
Your heart is a muscle in your chest that pumps oxygen-filled blood around your body.

SENSES
Your senses help you explore the world around you and send signals to your brain to help you understand it.

LUNGS
These two spongy bags in your chest are your lungs. They absorb oxygen from the air when you breathe in.

DIGESTION
The digestive system turns your food into fuel to keep you up and running, then gets rid of the bits you can't use as waste.

SKIN AND NAILS
Your skin keeps you warm and protects your squishy insides. You have 22 square feet of it altogether.

BONES
Your skeleton forms a frame that keeps you upright. You have 206 bones altogether!

MUSCLES
Your muscles help you walk, lift things, eat, and breathe by tugging on your bones to move them.

BUILDING BLOCKS OF LIFE

Nucleus

Membrane

MAKING YOU YOU

Your body is made up of building blocks called cells, which all do different jobs from moving to fighting illness to helping you see light. Almost every cell contains DNA, which is the special code that makes your body unique. It's stored inside the nucleus, which is basically the control hub of the cell. Each nucleus has 46 chromosomes, which are each made of a single strand of DNA.

BONES AND MUSCLES

Your bones and muscles are essential parts of your body. Together, they keep you up and moving around. They also keep all your organs in the right places and protect them from harm. Use your scanner to discover how they work together.

BONE ARMOR

There are 206 bones in your body, and they form the framework that keeps you upright and human shaped. Your bones are coated with a tough shell called periosteum to make them strong.

Some bones, like your skull and ribcage, perform extra-important roles of protecting your vital organs.

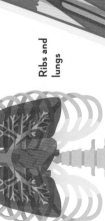

Skull and brain

Ribs and lungs

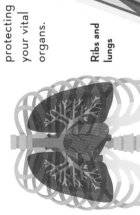

MUSCLE MOVEMENT

You have over 600 muscles in your body. Many of them are used to move your skeleton—and therefore you—around, but they also help you eat and breathe. They're made of long, stringy fibers that tense and relax to move your limbs.

When you bend your elbow, for example, the bicep (the muscle in your upper arm) pulls the bones together. When you straighten it out again, your tricep (the muscle on the back of your upper arm) pulls the bones apart.

Use your scanner to see how it works.

BONES / MUSCLES

Relaxed muscle

Contracted muscle

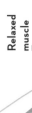

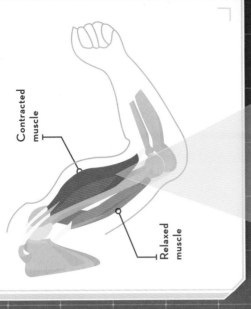

Contracted muscle

Relaxed muscle

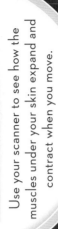

CONTRACTED / RELAXED

Use your scanner to see how the muscles under your skin expand and contract when you move.

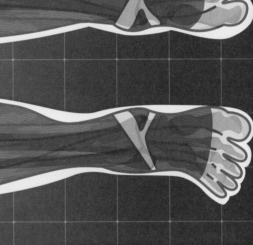

JOINTS

In order for your muscles and bones to work together, your skeleton is linked together with joints.

Ball and socket joints, like your shoulders, let your bones move in all directions.

Hinge joints, like your elbows and knees, work a bit like a door opening and closing.

Pivot joints, like in your neck, help you to rotate from side to side.

Ball and socket

Hinge joint

Pivot joint

BLOOD PRODUCTION

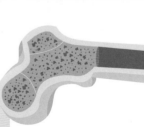

Inside your bones is bone marrow, a spongy substance that produces blood cells.

Blood cells carry oxygen around your body to power the cells within. They also fight germs and disease so that you stay healthy.

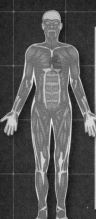

THE HEART

Your heart is located in your chest and protected by your ribcage. Even though it's only as big as your fist, the heart is one of the most important organs you have. It keeps you alive by pumping oxygen-rich blood around your body.

CHAMBERS / MUSCLE

Artery walls have to be very springy and elastic to cope with high-pressure blood from the heart.

1/3 cup of blood is pumped around your body with every heartbeat—enough to fill an egg.

Blood comes back to the right atrium and ventricle through your **veins**, then heads to your lungs.

CARDIAC CYCLE

PUMPING / FILLING

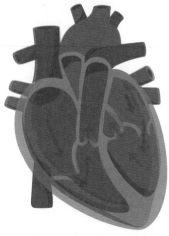

The cardiac cycle is basically how your heart contracts and relaxes in the space of one heartbeat. When the chambers of your heart are relaxed, they fill with blood. The heart then contracts to push it out into your arteries.

The left atrium receives blood full of oxygen from your lungs and sends it around the body through your **arteries**.

The walls of your heart are made of powerful muscles. They open and squeeze closed to push blood around your body.

BLOOD

Blood carries oxygen from the lungs around the body, and brings carbon dioxide waste back to the lungs so you can breathe it out. It also carries disease-battling antibodies and much more. So you could say it's pretty important!

FACTS

NUTRIENTS

Blood carries nutrients and minerals around the body to nourish your cells and give them the energy they need to keep you up and running.

BLOOD TYPES

We all have one of eight different blood types, which are tailored to protect our immune systems. The world's rarest blood type is AB–.

PLASMA

Plasma is the liquid that carries blood cells through the vessels. It's around 95% water but also contains nutrients, hormones, and waste products.

HEALING

Activated platelets

Platelets

Tiny platelet cells cluster around wounds and stick together, making scabs to stop bleeding.

DEFENSE

White blood cells detect germs, then attack them with antibodies. See page 21 to find out more.

CELLS IN ACTION / BLOOD FLOW

FUELING YOUR BODY

Oxygen

White blood cells

Red cells carry oxygen from the lungs to cells around the body.

The valves in blood vessels act like trapdoors to stop blood flowing backward toward your heart.

7

THE LUNGS

Your lungs soak up oxygen from the air you breathe, and send it around your body through your blood. You need the oxygen to turn food into energy and keep your cells alive. Your lungs then expel the waste gas, carbon dioxide, when you breathe out.

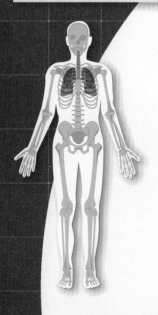

Bronchi split into lots of thin tubes called **bronchioles**, which pass oxygen to your blood through **alveoli** sacs.

BREATHING

IN / OUT

When the diaphragm moves down, your lungs get bigger, pulling air in. When it moves up, it squeezes your lungs, pushing air out.

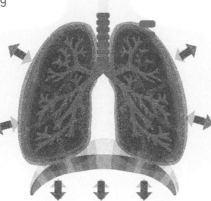

OXYGEN EXCHANGE

Alveoli are small sacs of air at the end of your bronchioles. They're wrapped in tiny blood vessels called capillaries that absorb oxygen from the air and pass it into your bloodstream to go around the body.

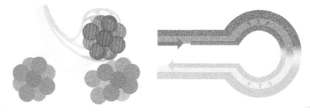

Air travels to your lungs down **the trachea**. There, it splits into two smaller tubes called **bronchi**.

The **diaphragm** is a stretchy membrane that makes your lungs bigger and smaller, helping you breathe.

Your lungs are protected by the strong bones of your ribcage. You have 24 ribs in total: 12 on each side.

FACTS

PHLEGM AND BOOGERS

Phlegm is mucus that builds up in the airways, whereas **boogers** build up in your nose. Both stop your airways getting clogged with dust and dirt that you might inhale.

COUGHS AND SNEEZES

Coughs and sneezes are the body's way of getting rid of unwanted particles in your airways, like dust or phlegm. After a deep breath in, your lungs squeeze out a sharp blast of air to dispel the blockage.

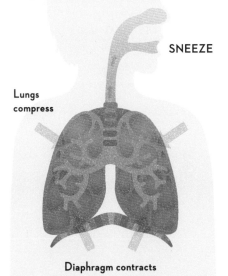

Sneezes travel up to 100 mph.

SNEEZE

Lungs compress

Diaphragm contracts

HICCUPS

Sometimes, your diaphragm tightens suddenly, making air rush into your lungs and snapping your vocal cords shut. The "hic" sound this makes is what we call hiccups.

SEEING YOUR BREATH

On cold days, the water in the air you exhale changes from water vapor, a gas, to tiny liquid droplets. This causes fog, and is why you can "see" your breath when it gets chilly!

THE SENSES

You have five main senses that you use to understand the world around you: touch, taste, smell, hearing, and sight. Your body sends signals to the brain, which then turns them into messages that we can understand.

VISION

At the back of your eye is a layer called the retina. When light hits it, special cells convert it into signals which travel through the optic nerve to your brain. The brain turns that information into images you can understand, like what color the grass is, or what's happening on your TV screen.

SMELL

When you breathe in, tiny molecules from things around you (like socks or soap), get picked up by special sensory cells up your nose. These cells send signals to your brain, which identifies what you're smelling and whether it's nice or not.

SCRAMBLED SENSES

What happens when you stare at these images? Do they look like they're moving? They're actually still; it just looks like they're moving because your eyes are tricked into seeing lots of light, shadow, and color at once, so they don't know what to focus on and your brain gets confused.

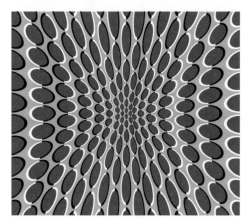 

HEARING

Sound waves make your eardrum vibrate. These vibrations travel to a spiral tube called the cochlea, which uses fluid and tiny hairs to send signals through your nerves to your brain. There, your brain unscrambles the signals to work out what you're hearing, like your favorite song, or your dad telling you it's dinnertime.

TASTE

Your tongue is covered in taste buds, which figure out if a food is salty, sour, savory, sweet, or bitter. This information goes to your brain through the nerves in your tongue, which also tell the brain what the food's temperature and texture are.

TOUCH

You have sense receptors in your skin that send messages to the brain. These messages tell you what you're touching and whether it's hard or soft, hot or cold, bumpy or smooth. You have most touch receptors in your fingertips, lips, and toes.

THE SKIN

The skin is your body's largest organ. It is tough and waterproof to protect your squishy insides from the wear and tear of everyday life. The blood vessels within make sure that you don't get too hot or too cold.

HAIR

Hairs grow from roots in **follicles** embedded deep within the skin. Your hair can grow 1/2 an inch every month.

NAILS

Bone

Nail

Epidermis

Your nails protect the sensitive nerves in your fingertips and toes. They grow 1/8 of an inch every month.

OIL

Your skin has special glands called sebaceous glands that release an oily substance called **sebum**. **Sebum** keeps your skin and hair soft. It can help protect against UV rays and even keep away some germs.

Follicle

TOUCH RECEPTORS

Hot and cold

Light pressure

Stretching

Deep pressure

You have millions of touch receptors that send signals to your brain through the nervous system. They help you figure out whether things are hot or cold, how hard they feel, and how stretchy or solid they are. Can you find them on the picture?

SURFACE

The upper part of your skin is called the **epidermis**. This layer is in charge of protecting your body, producing new skin cells, and keeping you hydrated. It also produces melanin, which is what gives your skin its color.

GOOSEBUMPS

When you get cold, the hairs on your skin stand up on end. The muscles this uses pull the skin up and make it bumpy. These "goosebumps" work better in furry animals, as this raised hair traps a layer of warm air close to the skin to keep them cozy. We're just not as hairy as them!

Use your scanner to see how the hair moves.

SWEAT

Feeling sweaty can be an uncomfortable sensation, but sweat is a good thing. It's produced by your skin to cool you down as it evaporates.

Blood vessels

CELLS

The cells in your skin form at the base of the epidermis and rise to the top, where they form the very top layer. These cells are flattened, then shed away. We shed 50,000 flakes of skin per minute!

FAT

Underneath your skin is a layer of fat that helps to keep you warm and stores energy for your cells to use.

BRUISING

When blood vessels get damaged and break, the blood gets trapped under your skin and forms a purpley mark.

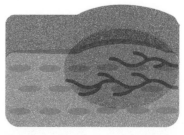

NERVES AND THE BRAIN

The nervous system is a network of nerves that runs through your whole body, from your head to your toes. The brain and spinal cord are the most important parts, forming a sort of highway for important information to travel around at over 267 mph. That's the length of the Grand Canyon every second!

NERVES

Nerves are encased in a tough, flexible coating that protects the fibers inside. These fibers carry messages to and from your brain and the rest of your body.

NEURON

Neuron is the name for a single nerve cell. It has up to 10,000 arms. The small arms receive signals from other neurons, and the long branch in the middle (called the **axon**) sends them out around your body.

THE BRAIN

The brain controls your actions and behavior. Your nerves send signals back to the brain from your sensory glands, which helps you to understand what's going on around you. This still happens even while you're asleep.

MOTOR - Spanning the top of your brain is the part that controls your muscle movements by sending signals to them through your nerves.

TOUCH - Your **parietal lobe**, in the middle of your brain, receives and interprets touch signals from your skin.

SIGHT - Your **occipital lobe**, at the back of the brain, is the part that receives signals from your eyes and turns them into recognizable images, enabling you to see.

THINKING & SPEECH - Much of your thinking is done in the **frontal lobe**, which helps you make decisions. It also contains **Broca's area**, which stores your vocabulary and helps you understand grammar and tone.

UNDERSTANDING - **Wernicke's area** helps you to process and understand language and what words mean.

MEMORY & HEARING - The **temporal lobe** receives signals from your ears and searches your memory to work out what you're hearing. It also contains your short-term memory and helps you smell things.

STEM - The **brainstem** is how your brain links to your spinal cord, enabling you to breathe, digest food, and keep your heart pumping blood around your body.

CEREBELLUM - At the back of your brain is the **cerebellum**, which helps you to balance. It also controls your spatial awareness, ensuring that you don't bump into anything.

SYNAPSE

A **synapse** is the gap between two neurons. Electric signals cannot cross it, so the axon has to diffuse a special substance to the next neuron.

REFLEX REACTIONS

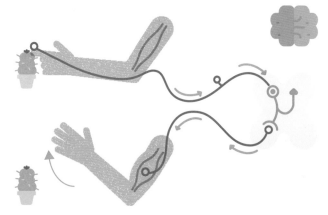

Reflexes are automatic reactions that help you avoid harm, like when you accidentally touch something very hot and move away quickly. This works by sending an instant message from your touch receptors along your nerves to your bicep, which moves your hand away. Another signal is then sent to tell your brain what just happened after you have already moved.

DIGESTION

Digestion is the process of your body breaking food down into tiny pieces and liquids that it can use. This process starts when you eat. The food travels down your esophagus to your stomach, then your intestines, and finally leaves in the form of pee or poop.

Digestion starts before you even take a bite. When you see and smell food, your **salivary glands** start to pour out saliva (spit) to help break down your meal and make it easier to swallow the food. When you do bite into your food, your teeth grind it into small pieces.

The pieces mix with saliva, then your tongue pushes it into a soft lump called a **bolus** and moves it to the back of your mouth. When you swallow the bolus, it goes down your **esophagus**, which is the long tube connecting your mouth to your stomach.

A process called **peristalsis** happens here, which means that the muscles in your esophagus ripple to push the food down your throat.

TEETH

Incisors cut and chop food. You have two on either side of each jaw.

Sharp, pointy canines rip and tear at tough food.

Molars have a flat surface to crush and grind your food.

When food reaches your **stomach**, the acid there breaks it down even farther with the help of the stomach's strong muscles which mix it all up.

Your **pancreas**, like the liver, helps to break down nutrients such as protein so that your body can absorb them.

Your **small intestine** is covered in tiny **villi**, which look a bit like fingers. They speed up the process of food being absorbed by your body.

Your **liver** is a large organ that extracts nutrients from digested food and passes them to your cells. It also produces a green liquid called **bile.**

The bile produced by the liver is stored in your **gallbladder**, where it gets released into the small intestine to break down fats.

Once your food can't be digested any farther by your small intestine, it heads to the **large intestine.** Water is absorbed, but the rest comes out as poop.

URINARY SYSTEM

Did you know that your body has its very own waste disposal system? Once food and drink have gone through the digestion process, anything left over has to leave your body. Use your scanner to see how your urinary system makes that happen.

The **medulla** inside your kidney filters the waste from your blood, and turns it to urine.

Blood enters through the vessels.

Urine travels out through your ureter.

KIDNEYS

Your **kidneys** work around the clock to remove excess water, salt and poisonous waste from your blood. This waste is then turned into **urine** (pee), and transferred to your bladder through a tube called the **ureter**. Meanwhile, the now-clean blood is sent back into your body.

Urine is stored in your bladder until you use the bathroom. The bladder is the size of a plum, but when full, can stretch to the size of a grapefruit.

LIFE CYCLE

On average, humans live for around 75 years. In that time, our bodies change a lot as we age from baby to adult, and continue to change as we grow older. This happens with the help of the trillions of cells that make up our bodies.

IN THE WOMB

While a baby is in the womb, it receives nutrients from its mother via the placenta, which filters them from the mother's blood.

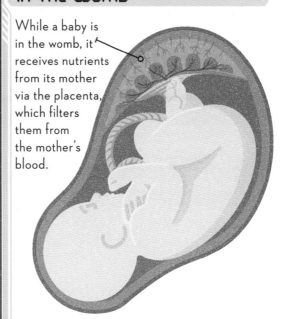

After eight weeks of growing in the womb, the embryo becomes a fetus. It continues to grow, recieving food, water and oxygen through the placenta. After around nine months of pregnancy, the now-grown baby is born.

CELL DIVISION

When an egg is fertilized, the process of **cell division** starts. The cell splits into two, then four, then eight and so on until an **embryo** is formed. This is the first stage of human development.

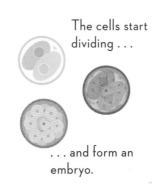

The cells start dividing . . .

. . . and form an embryo.

BIG CHANGES

BABY / ADULT

Babies have 300 bones, which fuse together so you have 206 as an adult.

Your body grows taller, and your bones get longer and fuse together.

You gain muscle during puberty, and these continue to develop afterwards.

When you're going through puberty, you gain more fat mass as your body grows upwards and outwards.

The spongey material between your bones gets worn out, shrinking your spine, and making you shorter.

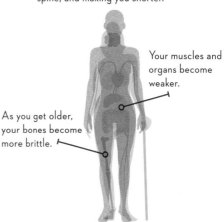

Your muscles and organs become weaker.

As you get older, your bones become more brittle.

CHILDHOOD
As a child, you are always learning as much as you can about the world around you so you can adapt and grow. You learn to walk, talk, and make friends.

ADOLESCENCE
As you grow up, your body changes. You grow taller and develop more muscle mass and fat as your body changes shape. Your behavior will start to change too as you begin to grow more independent and figure things out for yourself. This is a process known as **puberty**.

GROWING OLD
As you age, your cells break down. This is why adults might have more gray hair and less energy. They might move more slowly, and have worse hearing and eyesight.

HEALTH AND ILLNESS

Did you know that your body has its own set of superheroes? Much of your body works to keep you up and running, but there are some special defenses that are constantly working to protect you from illness. Use your scanner to find out more.

FRONT LINE DEFENSES

Before germs even get inside it, your body is already putting up defenses against them. You'll see these things every day—but did you realize just how important they are?

TEARS

Tears stop your eyes from drying out. They also help to focus light so you can see. If you get dust or dirt in your eye, tears carry it out safely to protect your delicate eyeballs.

EARWAX

Earwax is the sticky stuff that builds up in your ear. It traps dirt, dust, and bacteria. It also stops your ear from drying out and getting itchy.

MUCUS

Snot and mucus is produced by your nose and lungs to stop your respiratory system getting clogged with dust and dirt. Sometimes you sneeze or cough to get rid of the dust, firing out snot at speeds of up to 100 mph.

SKIN AND SWEAT

Skin basically acts like a waterproof coat for your body, protecting it from the outside world. It filters harmful sun rays, and cools you down with sweat.

SPIT

Spit helps to break down your food, but it also works to wash away the germs in your mouth.

INTERNAL DEFENSES

Your body is full of defense systems to keep you safe should any germs make it past the ones on the left . . .

Thymus – Found in the chest, this is where some white blood cells mature. It fades away as you grow up.

Axillary lymph nodes – These are in your armpits and filter lymph fluid, which contains infection-fighting white blood cells.

Peyer's patch – Found in your organs, these follicles regulate your intestines and prevent pathogens: disease-carrying organisms.

Appendix – Scientists don't know exactly what the appendix does, but it is thought to store good bacteria for your gut.

Tonsils and Adenoids – Your tonsils are at the back of your throat, where they trap and kill germs. Your adenoids are small lumps of tissue in your nose that do a similar job there.

Bone marrow – This is found inside your bones. It produces red and white blood cells to attack germs.

Spleen – Your spleen attacks bacteria and germs. It also stores red blood cells.

Inguinal lymph nodes – Found in your groin, these work with your axillary lymph nodes to filter your lymph fluid.

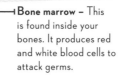

WHITE BLOOD CELLS

White blood cells are important because they detect and attack germs and diseases. There are several different types, which can renew daily or last for years. Some fire antibodies at germs, while others swallow the germs whole.

STAYING HEALTHY

Exercising helps you keep healthy as it makes your heart pump faster, sending more oxygen, water, and food to your body.

VITAMINS AND MINERALS – Found mostly in fruits and vegetables, vitamins do different things. Vitamin C, for example, is found in oranges and helps your body to fight off illnesses.

PROTEINS – Protein is found in foods like meat, fish, beans, and eggs. Your body needs protein to build and repair itself, as your cells and muscles are made of the stuff!

CARBOHYDRATES – These are found in starchy foods like bread, pasta, and potatoes. They provide a quick burst of energy and help you stay full.

CALCIUM – Calcium can mostly be found in dairy products like milk and cheese. It keeps your bones and teeth strong and healthy.

FATS – Found in foods like chocolate and meat, fat is good for you in small amounts as it stores energy and protects your organs.

INDEX